The Mass Media and the Dynamics of American Racial Attitudes

PAUL M. KELLSTEDT
Texas A&M University

List of Figures

years before, they did not even fight in the same units in the armed forces. They do not participate equally in the selection of the government officials who preside over both groups. Perhaps most ironically, though they worship the same God, cherish the same scriptures, and cling to the same cross, they do not attend the same churches.

These societal divisions were perfect reflections of American public opinion on race and civil rights, which had a distinctly segregationist, nonegalitarian flavor to it. Indeed, a 1942 survey revealed that only 41 percent of all Americans believed that black and white soldiers should serve together in the armed forces. Only 55 percent agreed that a black man could be just as good a soldier as a white man. Only 42 percent agreed that "Negroes are as intelligent as white people." The perceived differences between blacks and whites are hard to exaggerate, as only 36 percent believed that "Negro blood is the same as white blood." In addition to these strikingly prejudicial sentiments, the bulk of white Americans preferred to maintain distance between the races. Fifty-one percent claimed that streetcars and buses should be segregated. Fifty-five percent favored active job discrimination. Sixty-eight percent believed that white and black children should go to segregated schools. When it came to restaurants, 69 percent favored separate facilities, and fully 84 percent wanted segregated neighborhoods. This complex of attitudes existed in an atmosphere of denial that race was even a social problem worth addressing, as three Americans in five said that "Negroes are getting all the opportunities they deserve in this country."[1]

Indeed, southern society in 1950 was not so different from southern society in 1865. Eighty-five years after the Thirteenth Amendment to the Constitution ended slavery, things had not changed all that much for blacks in America. Blacks were still concentrated disproportionately in the South. There, blacks still tended to live in rural rather than urban areas. In absolute terms as well as in comparison to whites, blacks remained poor. In spite of the language of the Emancipation Proclamation, blacks were considered subhuman by most whites, and the society's laws and customs reflected this derision. Discrimination against blacks was more than tolerated; in many cases the law required

[1] These examples all come from surveys conducted between 1942 and 1946, and are reprinted in Cantril 1951.

it. For example, it was against the law in most southern states for blacks and whites to attend the same public schools and universities. In most places in the South, blacks were not allowed to participate in electoral politics. In nearly every case where the interests of blacks and whites came into conflict, the scales of justice were unfairly tilted in favor of whites. The testimony of blacks in court was typically discounted simply because whites controlled the justice system. Eighty years of freedom had not produced equality of any sort – not equality before the law, not economic equality, and, as the survey results just reported confirm, certainly not equality in the eyes of the American public. And eighty years of freedom had not even produced much movement toward those goals. Although slavery was gone, blacks were in almost every respect second-class citizens.

The year is 2000. Southern society is not as distinctive as it was a half-century ago. Many blacks have migrated to the northern cities in search of better-paying jobs. Many whites from the North have migrated to the South, and the formerly agrarian-dominated region is now one of the centers of America's economic growth. Beliefs about the innate inferiority of blacks are now dismissed as racist – witness the recent reaction to the controversial book *The Bell Curve*, which purported to show racial differences in intelligence but was quickly labeled pseudoscholarship thinly masking a racist political agenda. Public policy debates that focus on the role of blacks in society have evolved considerably; whereas in the past the debates revolved around whether discrimination *against* blacks should be allowed, the debate today centers on the question of whether discrimination *in favor of* blacks (in the form of affirmative-action policies) should be allowed. And it is not just the policy debates that have changed; government policies themselves have changed. The Civil Rights Act of 1964, the Voting Rights Act of 1965, and the Fair Housing statutes enacted in 1968 have given blacks the legal equality they formerly lacked. Legal segregation is a thing of the past, presumably never to return. The United States Supreme Court has made this clear in decision after decision. Laws and policies that discriminate on the basis of race are deemed "suspect" by the court and demand "strict scrutiny." Laws that either explicitly or in effect forbid black political participation have given way to full black participation in the polity, and today blacks actually participate at higher rates than whites, once socioeconomic status is controlled for.[2] Although blacks are still disproportionately poor compared to whites, the gap has narrowed. And the expansion of the welfare state has provided a safety net for blacks (as well as whites) who cannot yet achieve the American Dream on their own.

These shifts, unsurprisingly, have been accompanied by – or, in some cases, caused by – a sea change in American public opinion. The percentage of Americans favoring integrated schools rose from 32 percent in 1942 to 96 percent in 1995. The last time a pollster asked about segregated streetcars and buses, in 1970, fully 88 percent of Americans favored integration. The percentage of people favoring job discrimination has revealed a similarly dramatic movement: a 1972 survey showed that 97 percent preferred giving blacks an equal chance to get good jobs. Over the past half-century, clearly, a wave of egalitarian, antidiscriminatory sentiment – at least in principle – has swept over the American public.[3]

What happened in the last half-century that did not occur in the eighty or so years before that? To be sure, it is hard to exaggerate the profound change in American racial politics over the past fifty years, and this change is all the more remarkable given the equally profound lack of change over the previous eighty years. It is obvious that these societal shifts have occurred on several levels. The first level is that of public opinion. White society did not accept blacks as full partners in the American experiment in 1950, but at the turn of the millennium (with few exceptions) it does. In addition, the public's preferences have evolved with respect to the proper role of government in ensuring that blacks have access to the American Dream. Whereas whites formerly viewed government as a mechanism to insulate white society from blacks, today government is seen, at least in the minds of many, as a tool to protect minority interests from discrimination.

But perhaps the most significant change in American racial politics has occurred at the level of the national debate itself. In 1950,

[2] See Verba, Schlozman, and Brady 1996. It is true that blacks vote less frequently than whites and donate less money to campaigns than whites, among other forms of participation. This masks the fact that these differences are more than completely accounted for by the different socioeconomic standings of blacks and whites today. For example, middle-income blacks are more likely to vote than middle-income whites.

[3] These examples are from Schuman et al. 1997.

American society was struggling with the concept of the innate worthiness of blacks. By the mid-1950s, with the *Brown v. Board of Education* decision serving as the catalyst, the debate shifted to the issue of government actively discriminating against blacks by enforcing segregation. (Is "separate but equal" a good thing? Is it consistent with the Constitution? Can it be implemented?) In the 1960s, the debate shifted again, to the issue of governmental protection of blacks from discrimination in the private sector (such as public accommodations, employment, and housing). In the 1970s, the public discussion focused on the legitimacy of activist government policies like busing to end segregation in schools. And in the most recent period, debate has centered on the issue of affirmative-action policies that give preferences to blacks and other minorities in an effort to compensate for past discrimination or to ensure diversity in the workplace.

BLIND SPOTS: WHAT DON'T WE KNOW?

The scholarly literature on race in American politics is enormous, encompassing analyses that bridge such disciplines as economics, sociology, political science, public policy, and cultural studies. But the literature on race, vast though it is, has not produced much in the forms of theory or evidence on the role that the mass media have played in the evolution of race politics (or, more specifically, in public opinion) in the twentieth century. Our understanding of how the mainstream press has covered race – and especially how that coverage has evolved in anticipation of, in the middle of, and in the wake of the civil rights movement – is practically nonexistent. This despite the fact that nearly every scholar who has studied the politics of race would concede that the media have helped shape the course of race politics. On the face of it, few would deny that press coverage was critical to the unfolding civil rights drama of the 1950s and 1960s, for example. Most of the key events of the movement, after all – desegregation battles in Little Rock and elsewhere, bus boycotts, freedom rides – took place in communities that few non-southerners would have known about were it not for the national press. And yet the role played by the media in the unfolding drama of race in America has largely been ignored by scholars.

The literature on public opinion on race in America is similarly vast. Quite literally, decades of scholarly research have focused on the important question of why some Americans are racial liberals and others racial conservatives. Two leading theories have emerged, one focusing on the role played by overarching ideology, the other on the role of prejudice.[4] Scholars who have pursued the connection between ideology and racial attitudes have seen policy preferences on race, in the main, as a function of larger considerations about the proper role of government in American society. Citizens predisposed to believe that government cannot help solve society's problems will straightforwardly oppose governmental action in the case of race, whereas citizens who believe government can be an active part of the solution will tend to favor governmental action to level the playing field between white and black Americans.[5]

Another set of researchers has identified some form of racial prejudice (or the absence of it) as the leading factor that causes Americans to oppose or support liberal racial policies. These studies paint a very different picture of American public opinion, one that continues to be tainted with racial prejudice. In this view, when it comes to explaining why some Americans support or oppose liberal racial policies, ideological considerations are dwarfed by prejudice – and these ideological considerations are sometimes, in fact, merely convenient and "politically correct" covers for prejudice. Those individuals who harbor racial

[4] There are actually at least two other plausible explanations, though they are considerably less common in the academic literature. The first revolves around the concepts of group conflict and self-interest. The core idea here is that attitudes toward groups are a function of competition in the individual's environment and arise out of self-interest and a realistic conceptualization of intergroup conflict. This dates back at least to the political scientist V. O. Key (1949). For more recent examples, see Bobo 1983 and Giles and Evans 1986. Another theory, focusing around positions of social dominance, suggests that individuals in a dominant societal position seek to maintain that dominance; hence, whites will adopt policy views consistent with their historically dominant position over blacks in a social hierarchy. This is not a function of prejudice, but of a desire to maintain a position of power. See Sidanius et al. 2000 and the citations therein.

[5] The list of scholars endorsing this view is extensive. Most prominent among them, though, is the political scientist Paul Sniderman. See, for example, Sniderman and Carmines 1997; Kuklinski et al. 1997; Sniderman and Piazza 1993; Sniderman et al. 1991; and Sniderman and Tetlock, 1986a, 1986b. Often, in this literature, the notion that ideology determines racial policy preferences comes across mainly by implication, as competing theories are dismissed as *not* causing racial policy attitudes. Ideology, then, tends to be the only explanation left standing.

prejudice overwhelmingly oppose liberal government policies on race, and those without prejudice tend to support those same policies.[6]

This debate is serious, substantive, and likely to rage on for years to come. The variation that these scholars seek to explain – why some individuals are racial liberals and other individuals are racial conservatives at a given point in time – represents something that is important to society. But the intense nature of the debate obscures the fact that variation *among different individuals* is not the only source of variation worth explaining. In our zeal to explain the differences between liberals and conservatives, another kind of variation has been almost completely ignored. For in addition to zeroing in on variation among individuals at one point in time, as this literature has exclusively done, scholars could also ask questions focusing on variation *over time*. As it stands, our understanding of public opinion on race is excessively static, wrongly assuming fixed attitudes that cannot and do not change.

As a scholarly community, we have very little sense of how, as a whole, American racial policy preferences have varied over time. Indeed, we have almost no sense of whether they have or have not varied at all. Has American public opinion become more liberal on matters of race? More conservative? Or has it moved in both conservative and liberal directions at different points in time? Do racial policy preferences in the aggregate, over time, move in roughly parallel fashion, with the public becoming more liberal (or conservative) on all facets of race policy simultaneously, or does each subissue in the domain of race politics have its own unique dynamics?[7] The scholarly community has no answers to these questions, largely because we have never asked them due to our preoccupation with individual-level variation.

In turn, we have little sense of the causal dynamics that underlie any over-time change. If American racial policy preferences have varied over time, why have they done so? What forces have made American opinion more liberal (or more conservative) on race? By focusing

[6] Prejudice is often referred to, in these studies, as "new racism," or "symbolic racism," or "racial resentment." As with those focusing on ideology, the list of scholars emphasizing the role of prejudice in explaining racial attitudes is long. It is most closely identified, however, with Donald Kinder. See, for example, Kinder and Sanders 1996; Kinder and Mendelberg 1995; Sears 1988; Kinder 1986; Sears and Citrin 1985; Kluegel and Smith 1983; Kinder and Sears 1981; and Sears and Kinder 1971.

[7] Here I have in mind the famous articles published in *Scientific American* by Hyman and Sheatsley (1956; 1964). For more recent work in this vein, see Schuman et al. 1997.

exclusively on variation among individuals at one point in time, the scholarly community has neglected to identify and explain variation in the nation's racial policy preferences over time. And yet such variation is critical to understanding the ebbs and flows of race politics in America; indeed, given the centrality of race in American politics, we would not be exaggerating too much to say that identifying and explaining the over-time dynamics of racial attitudes would go a long way toward understanding all of American politics.

Here the two deficiencies of the literature on race in America – that it has neglected the role of the media and that it has been preoccupied with statics, not over-time dynamics – become related. The media's important role in shaping American racial politics can only be understood in a longitudinal framework. When we begin to appreciate this reality, we will find considerable power in explaining the over-time dynamics of American racial attitudes.

This book will make a connection that has been the source of a good deal of speculation, a great deal of polemic, but virtually no systematic analysis whatever – namely, the relationship between media coverage of race and American public opinion on race. In the process, the dynamic feature of racial politics in America will be emphasized. That is, the most interesting questions about race that have not been adequately addressed by the scholarly community revolve around how and why things today are (or are not) different then they were last year or ten years ago. Not surprisingly, then, the analyses in this book will have a distinctly time-series flavor. Given the focus on how and why racial politics has evolved over the last several decades, this is the most natural methodological approach. The end result will be a greater understanding of the sea change in racial politics that America has experienced over the last half-century.

The focus on over-time change will yield one other benefit as well. Although it is clear that both the national debates and public opinion have changed considerably over the past fifty years, we will also notice that most of these shifts have not been of the that-was-then-this-is-now variety. Indeed, despite the fact that the historical sketches that introduce this chapter show real change in race politics, our focus on time will prove that each of the years in between is an indispensible element of the story. Instead of viewing the changes as being akin to the differences between night and day, we will see that they are more like shifts in the tide, which rolls in, then out, and then back in again, leaving the beach a bit different each time.

In a sense, this book represents a revival of the first studies that examined racial attitudes over time, a tradition begun in the 1950s by Herbert Hyman and Paul Sheatsley in their famous articles in *Scientific American*, and continued more recently by Howard Schuman and colleagues.[8] This volume, though, benefits from recent advances in the study of public opinion – to be described in detail in Chapter 3 – that enable us to extract information from numerous opinion surveys at once, thus making a unified analysis possible. Instead of taking each survey item about every racial issue as something unique, I will strive to find communality among the various subdomains of racial politics. This new approach will empower us to tie the trends in public opinion to systematic causes like the national media in previously undiscovered ways.

A MACRO PERSPECTIVE

How and why do Americans' attitudes about race change? The illustrations that introduce this chapter show unquestionable and massive change in the span of roughly fifty years or less. These attitudinal shifts are surely, to a degree, a function of generational replacement. As older generations that were socialized in an America in which blacks were considered to be inherently inferior begin to die off and are replaced by generations that witnessed the struggles of Rosa Parks, Martin Luther King, Jr., and many others, surely the attitudes about the humanity of black people will change forever.

But how, if at all, do policy preferences about race change? It is worth noting that it has traditionally been assumed that such preferences do not change at all. In his famous 1964 treatise on public opinion, Philip Converse made the case that attitudes and policy preferences about race (along with attitudes about political parties) were the only stable and meaningful elements of a typical person's political "belief system." Perhaps because Converse's theory was so widely accepted, scholarly investigations into the shifts (and, implicitly, the causes of those shifts) in racial policy preferences have been rare. It has until

[8] See Hyman and Sheatsley 1956, 1964 and Schuman et al. 1997.

very recently been assumed that individuals' policy preferences on race were stable, even over the long run. Their attitudes on race, like their partisanship, were apparently a function of childhood socialization and education: they were the product of emotion, not cognition. Without trivializing the issue, one could say that the process by which a person acquires attitudes about race was, in many ways, seen as quite similar to the ways in which a person espouses a favorite baseball team. The process can essentially be boiled down to something not much more complicated than the fact of which team a person's parents rooted for.

But what if people do change their minds on race? What if the evolution of racial attitudes occur over the span of years and decades instead of over the course of generations? Perhaps still slow-moving, to be sure, and never to be confused with a fickle, moody public, what if there is evidence of shifts in racial policy preferences taking place at a rate that is too rapid to be accounted for by birth and death? What forces lead to such attitude change? And what does such change say about the politics of race in America, and indeed about American politics as a whole?

The answers, I believe, lie in the fact that Americans' attitudes about race are the product of their underlying political values – values that sometimes conflict with one another. Because different currents of the American ethos pull citizens in varying directions on the issue of race, with some core parts of their value system embracing government action while other parts simultaneously resist it, most Americans vacillate on the subject. That is, most of us see at least some truth in both sides of contemporary policy arguments about race policy. And, crucially, the American ethos is not a static, etched-in-stone body of ideas; it, too, is dynamic, with certain values becoming more prominent at some points in time, then, years or decades later, receding into the background, never eliminated from our consciousness but surely less prominent. In a sense, American attitudes on race resemble an internal tug-of-war between cherished values that conflict with one another – a struggle where one side gains ground over a period of time but the other side never truly loses, regaining strength and pulling back the other way.

But there is only one way to answer such questions definitively: go to survey marginals in search of stability and change in policy preferences on race. Once such shifts are discovered, we will need to generate entirely new theories of racial policy preferences, because the cross-sectional literature is largely predicated on the assumption of individual stability. We will draw from recent advances in the study of public opinion that focus on internal ambivalence, and will require the development of theories of political learning and information acquisition that will reveal much about the nature of public opinion itself. And, once we see the evolution in racial attitudes over time, we will hunger for an explanation for the trends we have discovered. This is where the twin gaps in the literature on race in America – not sufficiently dynamic, no explicit role for the media – will require us to develop new dynamic theories of racial attitudes that incorporate the role of the mass media.

The longitudinal approach taken in this book will produce different types of questions – and therefore different types of answers – than does the more traditional approach. I am advocating a perspective that focuses instead on over-time change in aggregate sentiment on racial policy preferences. This different perspective will show how the portrait of racial attitudes in America today differs from the similar portrait of a year ago, a decade ago, or a half-century ago – and, if successful, it will explain *why* as well. As such, the analyses to follow will resemble a motion picture more than a snapshot.

THE PLAN OF THIS BOOK

In the next chapter, I describe the evolution of media coverage of race in America. There, I introduce a new data base, comprised of every story written on race in *Newsweek* magazine between 1950 and 1994, along with a supplementary sample of *New York Times* stories. This data base will allow for a comprehensive analysis of previously unanswered questions such as: How, in terms of quantity and tenor, is media coverage of race today different – and how is it similar to – such coverage in the past? Have certain themes been more prominent at some times than others? Is there a discernable pattern in why coverage shifts? Is it driven by savvy political actors who inject symbols into public debate for their own advantage, or by dramatic events in the real world, or by something else?

In Chapter 3, I describe recent developments in the study of public opinion and examine their implications for racial attitudes over time in the aggregate population. I ask the questions: Have racial policy

The earliest of these studies were conducted in the 1950s. Perhaps more surprising than the conclusions, at the time, that blacks were portrayed in stereotypical and negative fashion is the fact that scholars *noticed* that black Americans were so portrayed. One of the first examples of studies of media portrayals of blacks was conducted by Audrey Shuey and her colleagues and published in 1953. Interestingly, it examined photographs, not stories, of blacks in six national magazines, scouring the photographs in both advertisements and news stories. The authors discovered that, overwhelmingly, black Americans were stereotypically depicted as "servants" in the advertisements and as "primitives, entertainers, and sportsmen" in the news articles.[4]

Of course, this was 1953. The idea that black Americans were portrayed as "servants" in advertisements then cannot be surprising to anyone who has cracked open a magazine from the period. Such a reader will invariably be confronted with pictures of, say, a black butler in a tuxedo serving a cocktail or a box of Chesterfield cigarettes to a white man in an easy chair. But at the end of the 1960s, the study by Shuey and her colleagues was updated by Keith Cox, who examined the advertisements in the same six magazines in 1967 and 1968. He found that the portrayal of blacks in below-skilled-labor positions had declined dramatically since the original study. Furthermore, blacks were increasingly shown in magazine advertisements in high-status positions, far exceeding the rates from the early 1950s. The stereotype of blacks as servants was apparently on the decline.[5]

But, as was to become characteristic of this literature, just as one scholar interprets changes positively, another comes along with the opposite spin. The challengers in this case were J. David Colfax and Susan Frankel Sternberg, who argued that Cox was far too charitable to the advertising industry in his interpretations. In particular, they criticized his definition of a "high-status" position, claiming that many of the positions Cox considered to be high status were really just new (and sometimes quite negative) stereotypes of black Americans. They wrote:

> Indeed, if the advertising image is to be believed, the black is a record star, an entertainer, a celebrity; if he is not one of these, he is a child, a woman, or a

[4] See Shuey, King, and Griffith 1953. The six magazines examined were *Time, Life, The Saturday Evening Post, The New Yorker, Ladies' Home Journal*, and *Colliers*.

[5] See Cox 1969; but for a different view, see Kassarjian 1969.

foreigner. As a male, he is in need of public or private charity, and he seldom if ever enjoys the occupational status of the whites with whom he is depicted. Missing from these ads are black families and black males, at work and at leisure – in short, the black American, rather than the black stereotype.[6]

As it turns out, whether the glass is half full or half empty depends on who's looking at it.

The subsequent literature documents this half-full-but-half-empty progress (and absence of progress) repeatedly. Whereas a more recent look at the images of blacks in national magazines by Paul Lester and Ron Smith presents the optimistic finding that stereotypical coverage of blacks is on the wane, a thorough review of the literature by Paula Poindexter and Carolyn Stroman shows quite the opposite. Focusing on television, they conclude that stereotypes of blacks continue to abound on television in the news and advertisements as well as in entertainment programming.[7]

The search for stereotypes has led scholars into some rather esoteric corners of the media universe. Raymond Rainville and Edward McCormick, for example, compared the treatment that black and white professional football players have received from announcers and color commentators. Football, until very recently, was a game where stereotypes flourished, especially about the intelligence of blacks and whites – which is why quarterbacks were almost always white. Rainville and McCormick's analysis of the play-by-play of sixteen games revealed that, indeed, black players got harsher verbal treatment after making a bad play, and less praise for a good one.[8] And, in recent work, White and Fuentes looked for, and found, stereotypical presentations of blacks in the cartoon section of papers, although they concluded that stereotypical depictions were declining.[9] Even in these more remote segments of the media world, scholars have found evidence of negative stereotyping of black Americans.

The most comprehensive study of press coverage of blacks that focuses on stereotyping was Carolyn Martindale's 1986 book *The White Press and Black America*. She examined a small sample of

[6] See Colfax and Sternberg 1972, p. 17.
[7] See Lester and Smith 1990 and Poindexter and Stroman 1981.
[8] See Rainville and McCormick 1977.
[9] See White and Fuentes 1997.

either the *quantity* or the *content* of press coverage of race. To be sure, it is valuable to recognize that stereotypes have existed for a long time, and that they are still around. Stereotypes may have particular political consequences, though it is critical to note that no study to date has even attempted a serious investigation of what those political consequences might be. But other facets of media coverage might also have consequences for the dynamics of race politics in America. This must be true. The only question is: what kind of coverage? The literature provides precious little guidance on this front.

At their worst, the existing academic studies of media coverage of black Americans collectively suffer from five serious deficiencies. First, the literature is insufficiently based on real media data and too often on mere speculation about what coverage actually has shown. Most of the studies that do look at actual data select extremely small samples of articles or issues to examine, and quite often those articles are not selected randomly. This means that the examined data run the risk of being unrepresentative.

The second shortcoming of the literature is perhaps a consequence of the lack of credible data: the literature is excessively normative. There is a rightful place for normative studies, of course. Normative prescriptions, though, ought to flow from solid, empirically based descriptions. Because these descriptions are lacking, the literature has a hand-wringing, self-flagellating tinge to it – and this is particularly true of the bulk of the literature that dwells on stereotyping. Too often, the conclusions seem to amount to the general conclusion that stereotyping is bad, and that there ought to be less of it.

Third, one of the criticisms of media coverage of race that appears in the literature – an exclusive focus on "crisis" events – is typified by the following comment in the published proceedings of a conference convened on the issue of race and the media: "What is not a crisis is usually not reported.... The news media...disregard the problems that seethe beneath the surface until they erupt in the hot steam that is a 'live' news story."[12] Such a criticism is undeniably true. Yet, ironically, the same accusation can be leveled at scholarly attention to media coverage of race: academic researchers have been disproportionately obsessed with coverage of "crisis" issues and, in the process, have

[12] Fisher and Lowenstein 1967, p. 4.

ignored day-to-day coverage of race. This is implicitly to assert that media consumers really only listen, watch, and learn when there is a crisis event. The trouble with this position is that it is assumed, not proven. And I suspect it is wrong. Every day when we read the morning paper or watch the evening news, we learn.

Fourth, far too many studies of press coverage are static, focusing exclusively on data from a single point in time. Most studies that look at actual coverage do not make any over-time comparisons at all. At best, they examine two time periods, perhaps separated by a decade or more, for a "before and after" glance. These minimal (and perhaps unrepresentative) samples of data are not truly dynamic analyses, where scholars systematically and deliberately incorporate the element of time into their comparisons. Thus, the scholarly community is left with little credible knowledge of whether the stereotypical themes have been covered at roughly the same rates over the past several decades. In the absence of such analyses, it has been assumed that coverage has been relatively constant. Is this assumption warranted? For example, we are told that the media stereotype blacks as poor. Has it always been the case? Or are such portrayals more recent phenomena? If these stereotypes have not always been prominent features of media coverage of race, when did they appear? Did they appear suddenly or gradually? To date, there are no answers to questions such as these.

Fifth, but perhaps most critically, the scholarly literature has provided no clear evidence that media coverage of race actually affects public opinion in any systematic way. Of course, this is an underlying assumption of research in this area – after all, if what the press says doesn't affect those who read, watch, or listen to it, then why study it? Despite the universality of this assumption, there is no evidence to substantiate these connections. For example, there are no studies documenting that those who consume what the media say about race believe anything different than those who are not media consumers. Nor are there any studies connecting shifts in media coverage of race – in its tenor, its emphases, or the like – to any shifts in public opinion over time.[13] In a scientific sense, then, media coverage exists as a

[13] And this stands in contrast to other areas of public opinion, such as presidential popularity, where explicit connections between media priming and framing have been shown to alter public opinion. See Iyengar and Kinder 1987 and Krosnick and Kinder 1990.

presumed cause without any demonstrated consequences and as a presumed consequence without any known causes.

In the rest of this chapter, I will outline a strategy to correct for these five shortcomings. It will be based on a systematic and large universe of stories in the national press. Moreover, it will focus on an entire half-century of coverage, observing both the crisis coverage as well as the messages conveyed in day-to-day stories about black Americans. In later chapters, this approach will – for the first time – allow for systematic hypotheses about both the origins of press coverage and the effects it has on public opinion.

A DYNAMIC APPROACH TO MEDIA FRAMES

Imagine for a moment that you are a scholar interested in the analysis of media coverage of race in America. Imagine further that you are unencumbered by the understandable problems that plague the literature – principally, the absence of a comprehensive data base of media stories on race over an extended period of time. In this hypothetical world, you have at your disposal all of the media data conceivable – presumably of the textual, audio, and video varieties – and that, furthermore, they are in readily analyzable fashion. The only limits are your creative ability to ask (and answer) interesting questions.

Where to begin? Like the kid in the candy store who thinks that everything looks delicious, you somehow have to decide what to try first. To what questions would you first want answers? For what concepts would you first want to develop measures? What kind of theory about cause and effect would you first want to answer?

I will pursue three main avenues of inquiry with the media data in this book. First, and at the most basic level, I believe it is important to document the *volume of coverage* that has been dedicated to racial issues in America. How much attention has been paid to racial issues in the mainstream press, and how has this level of attention varied over time? Presumably, media coverage peaked in the mid-1960s, at the height of the legislative push for civil rights. Did coverage increase dramatically then, or was it already at a high level before that? And how quickly, if at all, did it dwindle afterward? In the decades since the 1960s, have there been periods of resurgent interest in race politics on the part of the mainstream press? Metaphorically, when people listen to news about race, how loud is it in comparison to other salient issues?

The second major area of media coverage of race that I will focus on pertains to echoes of *core American values*. If race is "the" American issue, then it should not be surprising to find references – most often, subtle ones – to core American beliefs in news stories of race. In particular, for reasons relating to values that are prominent strands of American public opinion, I will search for mentions of two core American beliefs: *individualism* and *egalitarianism*. Because this book revolves around the over-time evolution of public opinion, facets of coverage that are directly related to key features of racial policy preferences – like values – seem especially relevant. That is, individualist and egalitarian frames in press coverage of race may be central to public opinion on race, particularly if racial policy preferences have their basis in these core values.[14] In Chapter 3, I argue that this is precisely the nature of racial policy preferences. Therefore, to the degree that opinion has its basis in values, tracking coverage that resonates with these values becomes important.

The final area of press coverage of race that strikes me as immediately relevant also has its origin in public opinion – namely, coverage that highlights the *disproportionate poverty* evident in the black community. Recent years have witnessed a proliferation of scholarship focusing on the relationship between attitudes about race and those about the welfare state.[15] But how much press coverage of race has even mentioned – to say nothing of emphasized – the real-world connection between race and poverty? What, when, and how much has the American public been learning about this connection?

This is my scholarly wish list. And, as noted, my idiosyncratic curiosities are surely a function of my interest in public opinion. That is, my interest is drawn to those areas of media coverage which are most likely to have a connection to American public opinion. The list of worthy topics a scholar might analyze – but which, in this book, I will not – is far longer. With a wealth of media data at hand, in-depth

[14] The word *frames*, in reference to the nature of media portrayals of an issue, comes from Gamson and Modigliani 1966.

[15] Much of the aforementioned literature on racial attitudes touches on this relationship obliquely, but for direct references see Abramowitz 1994, Gilens 1999, 1996, 1995, Carmines and Stimson 1989, and Stimson 1999.

particular, is a fecund area for symbolic coverage: over time, its use may have shifted – in particular, who is portrayed as the object of discrimination.

Later, I will begin to undertake many of these analyses, particularly those focusing on the sheer quantity of news, on the coverage of core American values, and on stereotypes like poverty. Others – especially those involving particular leaders, political issues, social problems, movement dynamics, and symbolic words – must wait for another day and other scholars with different but complementary interests.

I have emphasized the disparity between what we *assume* we know versus what we *actually* know, based on evidence, about the dynamics of media coverage. And I believe it is critically important that we test these assumptions. The results of such analyses will reveal much about American politics in the descriptive realm that is inherently interesting. When Americans consume news from the mass media, what are they learning about blacks – what they are like, what kind of people they are? From this perspective, one justification for this research is that many Americans, whites especially, learn a great deal about what they think blacks are like indirectly rather than directly, through the mass media rather than through (or at the very least in addition to) personal experience. What, exactly, are they learning?

It is equally important to underscore that these assumptions have never been examined. And with good reason. To subject them to empirical scrutiny would place extreme demands on the researcher. For example, it would require large amounts of textual data, which, because of the nature of the subject matter, must span several decades. As interesting as it might be to look into the dynamics of media coverage of blacks during, say, the 1980s and 1990s (when textual data became more readily available), there would be an obvious desire to see how such results would compare to coverage in the 1950s and 1960s. Moreover, the source of such material must be consistent over time. Finally, even if all of the data were available, determining a method for analyzing the text in a meaningful way presents a daunting task. In the next section I present a solution to these problems. My solution does not match my expressed ideal, where any and every research whim could be satisfied. At the very least, it represents a good first step in that direction.

THE *NEWSWEEK* DATA BASE AND *NEW YORK TIMES* SUPPLEMENT

No analysis that purports to speak of "the media" does justice to the breadth of this broad and constantly evolving institution. The lone exceptions to this generalization are those (relatively rare) works that deliberately set out to compare content across media. But these analyses, because of the sheer scope of the task, always compare media at a single point in time. For the longitudinal analyst, whose task is to collect data across large spans of time, this is even more problematic. The recent availability of data bases like Nexis, which contains a wide variety of print-news sources, and the Vanderbilt archives, which contains data from television news, is a positive development. However, for a project like this, which focuses on the evolution of racial politics over the last half-century, problems of data availability are obvious hurdles from the start, for no existing source stretches far enough back in time to permit the most informative types of analysis.

Therefore, the analyst interested in studying race in the media is left in something of a predicament. A wide variety of sources is available in electronic form from around 1980 onward. This permits more general conclusions about what "the media" are saying, but only for a severely restricted time period – a time period that does not cover the most interesting time in racial politics in recent history. Alternatively, the analyst can pick a single media source and attempt to supplement recent electronic data back in time. This strategy has the intended benefit of yielding data over a longer time span, but at the cost of examining a smaller slice of the possible media sources.

In this book, I have adopted a modified version of the latter strategy, focusing on a single news source for the last half-century but making comparisons to another source of data for the more recent time period in an effort to enhance measurement validity. The magazine *Newsweek* is the primary media source that will be used in these analyses.[21] For pragmatic reasons as well as issues of comparability, it was the best available source. For several decades, *Newsweek* has consistently had

[21] For those who are interested in analyzing these data further, all of the *Newsweek* stories are freely available in full-text format from my website, http://www-polisci.tamu.edu/kellstedt/.

a broad national circulation of over two million. Its audience is less highbrow than that of elite newspapers like the *New York Times* or the *Washington Post*. So an analysis of *Newsweek* is less susceptible to the criticism that only an elite few read it. And it is probably safe to say that *Newsweek*'s influence (like its circulation) has been relatively consistent over the years of interest. Contrast this with television (and hence television news), which was not widely available until the mid-1960s. Finally, the layout of *Newsweek* has not changed significantly over the period of analysis. Not surprisingly, the more recent versions of the magazine are considerably more slick and colorful in their graphical presentation. But the key sections of the magazine in the 1990s – the Periscope, National Affairs, Business and Finance, Perspective, and nearly all others – are identical to their predecessors from the 1950s. The articles tend to be of similar lengths, and the magazine has roughly the same number of articles per issue today as it had in the past. In short, on matters of format, I have been able to find no significant differences between current issues of *Newsweek* and issues from the 1950s.

For more recent years, media data are available from the Nexis data base. A total of 3,243 *Newsweek* articles from 1975 onward were obtained from Nexis.[22] This figure comes from a Boolean search in Nexis for at least two mentions of the words "Negro," "black," or "African-American" from 1975 through 1994.[23] This search criterion surely resulted in the retrieval of many irrelevant stories; any story that contains two or more mentions of, for example, black miniskirts would fit the search criterion. To avoid any possible contamination, these were eliminated by manually examining each of the 3,243 stories to see whether its content was manifestly about race in

[22] No other source was available in electronic form from Nexis as far back as 1975, with most sources coming on-line some time in the 1980s. For practical reasons, this makes *Newsweek* an attractive choice for a media source, because it minimized the amount of work needed to supplement the material that was readily available in electronic form.

[23] This search criterion was compared with several alternatives, including a Nexis subject search (subject = blacks), and was found to be superior. In particular, *Newsweek* defined which stories were about blacks very narrowly – too narrowly for my purposes. For example, stories about poverty that mentioned higher black rates of poverty were not classified by *Newsweek* as stories about blacks. Such stories obviously belong in my analysis, and therefore creating my own search criterion became necessary.

never has any scholar alleged that the American public does not have meaningful attitudes on race and mindlessly spouts the opinions suggested to them by the press. The manipulation hypothesis requires a public without real and substantive feelings and beliefs on race. But even Phillip Converse, pessimist that he was about the degree of sophistication of American public opinion, concluded that Americans' opinions on matters of race had consistency, both in cross-section and over time. Paul Sniderman and Thomas Piazza summarize the sentiment of every scholar in the field when they write that, on matters of race, Americans "have their feet, if not exactly set in cement, then at any rate firmly planted."[2]

Such a conclusion of media dominance would also, in my view, be unwarranted – an extreme interpretation of the data presented in this volume. In particular, such a conclusion would ignore two other prominent features of our findings. First would be the fact that we have consistently found other systematic forces *in addition to the media* to be relevant shapers of public opinion. Along with media coverage, in Chapter 4 we discovered that racial policy preferences are influenced by feedback from the policy system in a kind of thermostatic relationship. More liberal policies lead the public to decrease their demand for those policies. And welfare-state preferences also exert an influence on racial policy preferences. Further, in Chapter 5 we discovered that the merging of attitudes on race and the welfare state was, in addition to the media, caused by this same liberalization of racial policy. These causal influences are, quite simply, not consistent with the characterization of a puppet-like public.

The media-manipulation hypothesis also ignores what we have learned about where media coverage comes from. After all, in order for the media to be manipulative in any meaningful sense of the word press coverage itself could not be the result of other forces; it would have to be, in other words, that unmoved first mover. But it is not. The media seem to respond to the agendas of the most prominent American newsmakers – particularly the president of the United States, but also prominent movement leaders with their own agendas. This was particularly true, we have seen, in the case of the coverage of black poverty. But it is also true of coverage of egalitarian and individualist values. In

[2] See Converse 1964; Sniderman and Piazza 1993, p. 137.

other work, I have shown those types of coverage to be responsive to shifts in the economy and, again, to feedback from the policy system.[3]

What all of this rather clearly indicates is that the mass media are not, as some aficionados of conspiracy theories would like to suggest, the grand manipulators of public opinion, at least with respect to race politics. The media, to be sure, do play an important role in determining the shape and trajectory of public attitudes on race; but so, too, do other forces. And press coverage itself is a function of other, systematic forces. The media, in the end, are an important part of a system of influences that determine public opinion on race in America; but they are far from manipulators.

IMPLICATIONS FOR PUBLIC OPINION

Is public opinion rational? This is a question that public-opinion scholars have grappled with for years. And, you will notice, it is something of a loaded one. To answer in the negative is to cast serious doubt on the value of the democratic experiment. For to say that public opinion is not rational is to imply something unflattering – "irrational," "emotional," and "wrong" are adjectives that come to mind as antonyms. Normatively, that is a shaky foundation.

But it also seems to me to be the wrong way to evaluate public opinion. If we know that opinion on race is global, glacial, and tidal, we also know that opinion is not haphazardly moody. It is not subject to simple manipulations of slick politicians that cause abrupt reversals of opinion, lead to sudden reversals of public policy, and therefore undermine the stability of government. Because we know that public opinion is both slow-moving and a function of sensible, explicable forces, it is not random at its core. It is explainable. Perhaps that is rational enough.

A New American Dilemma?

The Swedish sociologist Gunnar Myrdal's famous work *An American Dilemma* (1944) set the stage, intellectually speaking, for the civil rights movement that was to begin a decade or so later. His treatise served as

[3] See Kellstedt 2000, esp. table 4.

the backdrop for the forthcoming social movement, and it clearly filtered down to the level of the popular debate. His thesis was that there existed a great chasm between America's egalitarian rhetoric and our clearly nonegalitarian treatment of blacks. On the one hand, almost all Americans were familiar with and proud of the country's egalitarian principles, which are embodied in the words and writings of their country's political heroes. "We hold these truths to be self-evident, that all men are created equal," proclaims the Declaration of Independence.

Equally self-evident was the fact that blacks were not considered to be a part of "all men" in the "all men are created equal." White Americans spoke the language of equality as eloquently as anyone, and these principles were for the most part uttered sincerely. Myrdal did not doubt this. But they were simply not thought to extend to blacks; and he noted that our prejudice was inconsistent with our liberal tradition. Myrdal was not exaggerating when he argued that it was hypocritical to subscribe to the abstract notion that all men are created equal but deny that blacks are a part of the equation. This was Myrdal's American Dilemma, and no one had identified the problem quite so clearly before he did.

But as this American dilemma has faded into the past, a new American dilemma has emerged to replace the old. Should American society endorse policies that attempt to compensate for the injustices of the past, or do such policies create problems bigger than the ones they purport to solve? Should society, either literally or in effect, make amends to its black members, or should society tell its black members to make it on their own? When faced with such a decision, most individuals will reflect on the options and pick the one most consistent with their core values. And that is precisely why this situation is so vexing. For in this case, one of America's core values – egalitarianism – prescribes activist government policies, while another – individualism – forbids them. This is the new American Dilemma.

A critical distinction between the old American Dilemma and the new is that the lines of division have changed. Before, America was divided into two groups of people, some of whom thought blacks deserved the full benefits of American citizenship, others of whom thought that blacks were inherently inferior beings. Today, the fault lines are not between individuals but within them. One part of most Americans cries out for compensatory justice, that our society must

Lester, Paul, and Ron Smith. 1990. African-American Photo Coverage in *Life*, *Newsweek*, and *Time*, 1937–1988. *Journalism Quarterly* 67 (Spring): 128–36.

Lipset, Seymour Martin. 1967. *The First New Nation*. Garden City, N.Y.: Doubleday.

Lipset, Seymour Martin, and William Schneider. 1978. The Bakke Case: How Would it be Decided at the Bar of Public Opinion? *Public Opinion* 1:38–44.

Martindale, Carolyn. 1986. *The White Press and Black America*. New York: Greenwood.

Mayer, William G. 1992. *The Changing American Mind*. Ann Arbor: University of Michigan Press.

McAdam, Doug. 1982. *Political Processes and the Development of Black Insurgency, 1930–1970*. Chicago: University of Chicago Press.

McClosky, Herbert, and John R. Zaller. 1984. *The American Ethos*. Cambridge, Mass.: Harvard University Press.

Myrdal, Gunnar. 1944. *An American Dilemma*. New York: Harper and Row.

Page, Benjamin I., and Robert Y. Shapiro. 1992. *The Rational Public: Fifty Years of Trends in Americans' Policy Preferences*. Chicago: University of Chicago Press.

Piazza, Thomas, Paul M. Sniderman, and Philip E. Tetlock. 1989. Analysis of the Dynamics of Political Reasoning: A General-Purpose Computer-Assisted Methodology. *Political Analysis* 1:99–119.

Poindexter, Paula M., and Carolyn A. Stroman. 1981. Blacks and Television: A Review of the Research Literature. *Journal of Broadcasting* 25 (Spring):103–22.

Popkin, Samuel L. 1994. *The Reasoning Voter: Communication and Persuasion in Presidential Campaigns*. 2d ed. Chicago: University of Chicago Press.

Quadagno, Jill. 1994. *The Color of Welfare: How Racism Undermined the War on Poverty*. New York: Oxford University Press.

Rahn, Wendy W., John Transue. 1996. "The Political Significance of Fear of Crime." *A Report to the National Election Studies Board of Overseers*.

Rainville, Raymond E., and Edward McCormick. 1977. Extent of Covert Racial Prejudice in Pro Football Announcers' Speech. *Journalism Quarterly* 54 (Spring):20–6.

Report of the National Advisory Commission on Civil Disorders. 1968. New York: E. P. Dutton.

Schuman, Howard, and Stanley Presser. 1981. *Questions and Answers in Attitude Surveys: Experiments on Question Form, Wording, and Context*. New York: Academic Press.

Schuman, Howard, Charlotte Steeh, Lawrence Bobo, and Maria Krysan. 1997. *Racial Attitudes in America: Trends and Interpretations*. Rev. ed. Cambridge, Mass.: Harvard University Press.

Sears, David O. 1988. Symbolic Racism. In P. A. Katz and D. A. Taylor, eds., *Eliminating Racism: Profiles in Controversy*. New York: Plenum.

Sears, David O., and Jack Citrin. 1985. *Tax Revolt: Something for Nothing in California*. Cambridge, Mass.: Harvard University Press.
Sears, David O., and Donald R. Kinder. 1971. Racial Tensions and Voting in Los Angeles. In W. Z. Hirsch, ed., *Los Angeles: Viability and Prospects for Metropolitan Leadership*. New York: Praeger.
Sears, David O., James Sidanius, and Lawrence Bobo, eds. 2000. *Racialized Politics: The Debate about Racism in America*. Chicago: University of Chicago Press.
Shuey, Audrey M., Nancy King, and Barbara Griffith. 1953. Stereotyping of Negroes and Whites: An Analysis of Magazine Pictures. *Public Opinion Quarterly* 17 (Summer):281–7.
Sidanius, James, Pam Singh, John J. Hetts, and Chris Federico. 2000. It's Not Affirmative Action, It's the Blacks: The Continuing Relevance of Race in American Politics. In David O. Sears, James Sidanius, and Lawrence Bobo, eds., *Racialized Politics: The Debate about Racism in America*. Chicago: University of Chicago Press.
Sigelman, Lee, and Susan Welch. 1991. *Black Americans' Views of Racial Inequality: The Dream Deferred*. New York: Cambridge University Press.
Skogan, Wesley G. 1995. "Crime and the racial fears of white Americans." *The Annals of the American Academy of Political and Social Science* 539 (May): 59–71.
Sniderman, Paul M., and Edward G. Carmines. 1997. *Reaching beyond Race*. Cambridge, Mass.: Harvard University Press.
Sniderman, Paul M., and Thomas Piazza. 1993. *The Scar of Race*. Cambridge, Mass.: The Belknap Press of Harvard University Press.
Sniderman, Paul M., Thomas Piazza, Philip E. Tetlock, and Ann Kendrick. 1991. The New Racism. *American Journal of Political Science* 35:423–47.
Sniderman, Paul M., and Philip E. Tetlock. 1986a. Symbolic Racism: Problems of Motive Attribution in Political Analysis. *Journal of Social Issues* 42(2):129–50.
1986b. Reflections on American Racism. *Journal of Social Issues* 42(2):173–87.
Stimson, James A. 1994. Domestic Policy Mood: An Update. *The Political Methodologist* 6(1):20–2.
1997. The Micro Foundations of Mood. In James Kuklinski, ed., *Citizens and Politics: A Political Psychology Perspective*. New York: Cambridge University Press.
1999 [1991]. *Public Opinion in America: Moods, Cycles, and Swings*. 2d ed. Boulder, Colo.: Westview Press.
Stimson, James A., Michael B. MacKuen, and Robert S. Erikson. 1995. Dynamic Representation. *American Political Science Review* 89(3):543–65.
Tarrow, Sidney. 1998. *Power in Movement: Social Movements and Contentious Politics*. 2d ed. New York: Cambridge University Press.